The CYCLE OF VICTORIOUS GIVING

Your Time, Your Talent, Your Treasure

STAN & LINDA TOLER

Beacon Hill Press of Kansas City
Kansas City, Missouri

ISBN 083-412-0992

Printed in the
United States of America

Cover Design: Michael Walsh

Library of Congress Cataloging-in-Publication Data

Toler, Stan.
   The cycle of victorious giving : your time, your talent, your treasure / Stan Toler, Linda Toler.
      p. cm.
Includes bibliographical references.
   ISBN 0-8341-2099-2 (pbk.)
   1. Stewardship, Christian—Church of the Nazarene. I. Toler, Linda, 1951- II. Title.

BV772.T63 2004
248'.6—dc22

                                                    2003025786

10   9   8   7   6   5   4   3   2   1

To Wilma Cole, a model of Christian stewardship
and without a doubt one of the
most generous people in the whole world!

CONTENTS

ABOUT THE AUTHORS

Stan and Linda Toler live in Oklahoma City. Stan, is senior pastor of Trinity Church of the Nazarene, and Linda teaches at Bethany Elementary School. The Tolers coauthored the book *Christmas Traditions* with their good friends Elmer and Ruth Towns. They have two sons: Seth, an Oklahoma City policeman, and Adam, a junior at Southern Nazarene University. They also have a Dalmatian named Marmaduke, who runs the house.

The Tolers may be reached via the following contact information:

Stan and Linda Toler
P. O. Box 892170
Oklahoma City, OK 73189-2170
E-mail: stoler1107@aol.com
Web site: www.stantoler.com

PREFACE

As a college student in 1971, I (Stan) discovered a life-changing book. It was written by the esteemed pastor of Pasadena (California) First Church of the Nazarene, Earl Lee, and his wife, Hazel. Its principles for victorious Christian living gave me valuable spiritual bearings. And I wasn't alone. *The Cycle of Victorious Living,* based on a study of Ps. 37, became a best-selling book for Christians who seek to apply biblical truths to their challenging lives. Dr. Lee spoke at our chapel service, and I was privileged to take him to the airport. During that short trip, the wealth of spiritual advice that he translated into the book poured from his heart. I listened intently to his every word and realized that he was a man who not only wrote about victorious living but also fleshed it out in every aspect of his life.

The Lees became walking examples of God's grace and peace during the Iranian hostage event that ended in January 1981. Their son, Gary, was one of the American hostages held for 444 days. And while their hearts must have been bursting with pain during his captivity, they faced their crisis with such spiritual and emotional victory that even the news media covering their plight was profoundly influenced. In fact, one of the reporters gave her heart to Christ as a result of her encounter with this godly couple.

I've always felt that the basic concepts of *The Cycle of Victorious Living* could be applied to a specific area of Christian living: Christian giving. Imagine my delight when my friend Steve Weber, director of stewardship ministries for the Church of the Nazarene, encouraged me to "go for it." The project was sealed in my heart when Bonnie Perry, director of Beacon Hill Press, said enthusiastically, "Amazing idea! Let's do it!"

When I shared the idea with my wife, Linda, she felt the same enthusiasm. We agreed that our version of *The Cycle of Victorious Living* would be a reflection of what we have learned about the "cycle of victorious giving," which has blessed our own lives during our 30 years of marriage and full-time ministry. That was the beginning of this book.

Some Christians choke on the very word *giving*, while countless others have made the discovery that *victorious giving* means *victorious living.* We're with the last group. Like others, early in our marriage we made a spiritual covenant to obey God's Word regarding our finances. In my book *God Has Never Failed Me, but He's Sure Scared Me to Death a Few Times* I write about putting Earl and Hazel Lee's principles into practice by making a giving pledge during a missions conference. That single incident turned into a way of life for Linda and me. Countless times, we have marveled at the way God has opened the windows of heaven on us and proved the "cycle of victorious giving" principles in practical and powerful ways.

Jesus wasn't afraid to talk about important issues—including the wise use of money. In fact, more than 2,000 verses in God's Word directly address finances. That's pretty important! Jesus knew that at the heart of our surrender to Him is our attitude about material things. We can't give Him just our bodies, souls, and minds. He must also have our bank accounts, our stock portfolios, and our material possessions. Of course, those gifts won't save us. Only His blood can save us, only the gift of His own life on our behalves. But the very act of giving proved that we were saved—that in gratitude for His giving, we turned our lives and living over to Him, to the one who can manage them with supernatural vision.

We don't have to look very far for proof that the "cycle of victorious giving" works. We need only to look in the mirror. It's worked in our home. We've made the wonderful discovery of God's blessing on our giving. We discovered it first as a young couple pastoring a small church and struggling to make a car payment and clothe our two sons. And we've discovered it in a daily and continuing way, as parents of grown children, living in a comfortable home, and starting to plan for the not-so-distant days of retirement.

And, may we add, we've seen the same evidences of God's blessing through difficult times of life-threatening illness as in days of recovery and active mega-ministry.

It works! This principle of *giving, receiving, and giving again*—the "cycle of victorious giving"—is not just a theory. It's a way of life—abundant life.

We pray with all our hearts that this book will make a life-changing difference in your Christian life.

ACKNOWLEDGMENTS

Special thanks to Jerry Brecheisen, Jeff Dunn, Deloris Leonard, Jonathan Wright, Laura Womack, and Pat Diamond for their creativity and editorial insight. Hats off to Bonnie Perry, Hardy Weathers, Mark Brown, Barry Russell, and Steve Weber for their encouragement to do this project.

INTRODUCTION

The Church has had an abundance of teaching on the subject of giving. From the airwaves to the printed page, a wealth of information is available. But in our judgment, some of the teaching has had a negative influence. Certainly God has promised to prosper His children. That's one of the long-term benefits of knowing Christ as Savior. He has promised to take care of His own.

But not in a cookie-cutter way.

He can bless us as much in a tent as He can in a temple. We can enjoy the abundance of His supply whether we're driving a new luxury car or a used car with over 100,000 miles on it. His wealth is unlimited—from real estate holdings to precious jewels. We used to sing a Sunday School chorus that summed it up: "He owns the cattle on the thousand hills, / The wealth in every mine; / He owns the rivers and the rocks and rills, / The sun and moon that shine."* He can give us whatever He wants, whenever He wants, and in whatever package.

More importantly, He gives what's best. In the beloved New Testament story, the prodigal son received all of his inheritance at once. But later on, his elder brother was enjoying a daily supply of good things, while the errant prodigal was living in poverty after squandering his wealth. (See Luke 15:11-32.)

God is concerned with *daily supply.* Jesus taught us to pray, "Give us *this day* our daily bread." For some, that supply will be parceled out in stock dividends and thriving business options. For others, it will come in smaller portions such as unexpected overtime at an hourly job or a surprise rebate on a purchase.

Either way, the riches of heaven are being applied to the residents of earth.

In the economy of God's kingdom, we don't give in order to get something back. We simply give because we love God. We give as an expression of our appreciation for His blessings and as an expression of our loyalty to Him. And in return, we receive sovereign benefits continually supplied in just the right amount for our spiritual good. Then, in return, we give back— we *recycle* God's blessings.

Prosperity is a gift from God, not a guarantee of Christianity. At times, poverty can be blessing. For example, out of her poverty Mother Teresa blessed the helpless and hopeless of India. She had little of the world's resources, but with what she had she ministered to untold thousands.

Like the Laodicean church in the Book of Revelation, "fat cat faith" can be a curse. The church in its luxury can miss out on the blessing of God's presence and purpose.

Christianity isn't about gold watches; it's about golden crowns—crowns of service that will one day be cast at the feet of a Savior who left the splendor of heaven to live homeless on the earth, a Savior who had everything but gave it all up so that we could enjoy the luxury of forgiveness and the priceless hope of a future.

This is a book about balance, about giving to *give*, not giving to *get*, about a victorious cycle of giving that will result in as much peace as prosperity, in as much wisdom as wealth, in as much living as luxury.

There are four main components to this "cycle of victorious giving." The first is *trust*. We trust to live. We commit our ways—including our finances—to the Lord and rest in His abundant supply. That in turn provides a vital connection to God.

The second is *commitment*. We commit to grow. We plant spiritual seeds in order to reap spiritual maturity. Our giving reflects our attitudes toward material things.

The third component is *delight*. We delight to give. Giving is an act of Christian community. It provides us with inner spiritual satisfaction. It enhances life—it does not impede it.

The fourth is *rest*. We rest to inherit. Giving reaps eternal dividends. God has promised a fabulous ending! When we make a commitment to His kingdom on earth, we're actually making an investment in eternity.

The Cycle of Victorious Giving

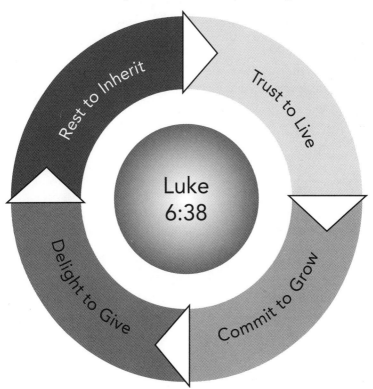

The "cycle of victorious giving" can be life-changing and life-freeing. Through these pages you will discover an exciting new way to look at both material blessings and spiritual blessings. You will be freed from negative attitudes toward money.

You will be freed to enjoy positive principles that God has given us to make us both financially and spiritually whole.

Get ready!

God does have a wonderful plan for your life. He wants you to enjoy the journey to heaven. He has already planted some fantastic promises in the road map of His Word. And He has provided enough resources along the way to keep you sustained and whole.

Open your heart to His lavish supply. Learn how He has already made an investment in your life. And learn how you can realize a guaranteed return on the investment you make in His kingdom.

In fact, the "cycle of victorious giving" is simply another step in the "cycle of victorious living."

TRUST TO LIVE

Giving Connects Us with God

Trust in the LORD and do good;
dwell in the land and enjoy safe pasture.
—Ps. 37:3

In 1971 Beacon Hill Press of Kansas City took a chance with a small book titled *The Cycle of Victorious Living*. More than 100,000 copies later, it is a classic by any definition.

I (Stan) was privileged to hear its author, Earl Lee, speak on the subject of his book the year it was published. After listening to him, I modified his "cycle of victorious living" to the "cycle of victorious *giving*," with a faith promise pledge during our annual missions conference. I felt impressed by God to give $100 as a pledge of faith. And at that time it certainly was a *faith* pledge. College expenses had put a colossal crimp on my finances. I paid the pledge promptly, but it took the last of my cash. After the offering, I was broke. Good old-fashioned worry weighed heavily on my mind.

Soon after, while I was working part-time as a barber at the North Court Barber Shop in Circleville, Ohio, my boss said he wanted to talk to me.

More worry.

"Stan," he began, "all the other barbers in this shop have a chance to get more tips and profits from the sale of hair products than you. But you're doing a great job! Here's a bonus of $100—just don't tell the others."

If it weren't for two things, I would have danced around the shop and hugged my boss's neck. First, back then students at the college I attended weren't allowed to dance. Second, pedestrians passing by the big plate glass storefront of the shop on their way to Risch's soda fountain probably wouldn't understand why I was hugging my boss.

God taught me something that day. I discovered that I could never beat Him in a giving competition. God honors obedience. And He loves it when we learn to trust.

Earl and Hazel Lee wrote,

> If faith is nothing apart from its object, the same is true of trust, for they are closely akin in meaning. The recommendation from Scripture is to lean hard on the Lord. He made heaven and earth. He calms the storms and stills the waves. His is the earth "and everything in it, the world, and all who live in it" (Ps. 24:1). He is the One on whom you lean—all your weight on all of Him! You feel lighter after casting your cares on the Lord. Once you find release through commitment and trust, leaning hard becomes another forward move in the cycle.[1]

Living in the Cycle

When you first learn to trust God—to lean hard on His power, His presence, and His provisions—you've entered the *cycle.* You have begun the journey of faith; you've made the wonderful discovery that God will not fail to keep His word. I (Stan) will never forget kneeling in a college chapel service and raising my hands in full release of all the fears that had haunted me since the death of my dad. As I entered the "cycle of victorious living," peace swept over my soul.

The first words of the Bible are "In the beginning God." It's the same in the "cycle of victorious giving." It begins with God—with who God is, with what He has promised, with what

He has already provided. In essence, you've begun your journey on the sunny side of life. The positively positive! You've leaned against the resources of the God of the universe, whose supply is endless.

The God of Abundance

Our friend Chuck Crow loves to tell the story of a company that sometimes puts on what they call "Lunch and Learn" seminars during the employees' lunchtime, dealing with a variety of physical and mental health issues. If the seminar lasts beyond the normal lunch hour, employees are supposed to get managerial approval to attend. He laughingly tells about a flyer that circulated not long ago that read, "Lunch and Learn Seminar: Who's Controlling Your Life? (Get your manager's permission before attending)."

No matter what the issue is in our lives, we must come to the same conclusion: God is our manager. He owns it all (Ps. 24:1), and that includes all our problems. He has immeasurable riches and lavishly gives to us from that abundance. Our material possessions are not ours after all. They belong to God. He simply lends them to us to meet our daily needs.

Granted, trusting God in that manner is contrary to human nature. Jesus warned us, "Do not let your hearts be troubled. Trust in God; trust also in me" (John 14:1). Ever since the events in the Garden of Eden, we've had the tendency to do things our way. We appoint ourselves CEO of our own lives and live by the faulty premise that our *decisions* result in our *provisions.*

We Can't Do Anything

So much of what God has promised can't be controlled by our efforts, including our salvation. Jesus said, "I am the way and the truth and the life. No one comes to the Father except through me" (John 14:6). Often we act as if God's guarantees had a line in small print that nullifies His promises unless we do all the work. Salvation's work has already been done. The price of redemption has already been paid. We live by *grace* through faith, not *grit*. Out of His abundance and love, God poured out His supply, giving us what we could not earn or buy.

Trusting God means believing what we cannot see. Heb. 11:1 states, "Faith is being sure of what we hope for and certain of what we do not see." He moves across the landscape of our lives, working miracles that we cannot envision or understand. The sun rises. The seasons evolve. Rain falls. Snow caps the mountaintop. Planets turn in their orbits. We don't understand how it all works; we just enjoy the benefits. And we believe that the Creator is in control of it all.

If God takes care of that, He can be trusted to take care of the details of our lives as well. Thomas G. Long commented,

> Ultimately, whether one serves God or wealth depends upon trust. The appeal to trust God is the goal of Jesus' picture of the birds of the air, which are fed by God even though they neither fret nor plan, and the lilies of the field, gloriously and colorfully clothed even though they have never touched a needle and thread. If God takes care of the birds and the wild flowers, Jesus promises, then surely God will take care of us. So, not only are we freed from compulsive anxiety about vain luxuries, we do not even need to worry about the basics, about food or clothing, because our God knows we need all these things (Matt. 6:31-32) and will provide."[2]

Trusting God is a reminder that He is CEO—and CFO (chief financial officer)—of our lives. Prov. 3:5-6 tells us, "Trust in the LORD with all your heart and lean not on your own understanding; in all your ways acknowledge him, and he will make your paths straight." By committing the details of our lives to Him—including our finances—we acknowledge spiritually that He is a loving and trustworthy Heavenly Father.

Knowing Our Source

Trusting God also verifies that He is the source of our supply. Deut. 10:14 states, "To the LORD your God belongs the heavens,

even the highest heavens, the earth and everything in it."
When you acknowledge that everything comes from Him, it
puts the ball in His court. The pressure is still on—but the pressure is on God, not you. You simply do the daily tasks of life, diligently, faithfully, and skillfully. He's in charge of the bottom line.

Moses didn't worry about water levels. He simply trusted God
to part the waters and get the Israelites through the Red Sea.

David didn't worry about proportionate height or strength
for his contest with the giant Goliath. He simply picked up a
stone and left the driving to God.

Joseph didn't worry about online courses on protocol or purity. He just depended on God's wisdom to run Potiphar's
household—and to run *away* from Potiphar's wife.

The woman who touched the hem of Christ's garment wasn't
concerned with keeping the rules of etiquette. She pushed
through the crowd and went directly to the source of her healing,
the Ruler of life and death.

The apostle Peter didn't worry about the laws of gravity. He
simply got out of the boat and started walking on the water toward the Master. Peter knew he could trust Jesus in the midst
of a storm.

Recently we saw a sign posted in a warehouse that should
be permanently engraved in all of our hearts. It read,

> Good morning. This is God.
>
> I will be handling all of your problems today.
>
> I don't need your help.
>
> So have a nice day.

Staying out of God's way is the key to having a great day!

The Giver of Perfect Gifts

God isn't a "finders keepers" Father. He's the giver of "every
good and perfect gift" (James 1:17). God so loved the world that
He gave! Every fiber of His holy being is filled with generous
giving. From the fragrance of the rose to the soft sands of the
beach, His only concern is to enhance the lives of His creation.

His greatest gift was His only Son. He gave His "only begotten Son" (John 3:16, KJV). Out of His love for us, God was willing to give the dearest and best of His possessions. "Only" is such a key word in this scriptural scenario. It reveals the height, depth, and width of God's love. No sacrifice was too great to provide a source of forgiveness and hope for us. The link is absolute: He loved; He gave. And we reap the eternal benefits.

That same cycle of giving can be realized in our lives as well. God promises to *supply* in response to our *service.* "Seek first his kingdom and his righteousness, and all these things will be given to you as well" (Matt. 6:33). There are several important principles to remember about His supply.

First: *We reap what we invest.* That is seen in all of life. In nature the harvest comes after the sowing. In football the touchdown comes after the run or the pass. In science the discovery comes after the experiment. The effort produces the effect.

It's the same in the spiritual realm. The Bible says, "The wicked man earns deceptive wages, but he who sows righteousness reaps a sure reward" (Prov. 11:18).

A seasoned citizen from our church was answering phones on a television show I (Stan) was hosting when a young lady called to ask prayer for her desperate financial situation.

Everet got the call and began to counsel the young lady. "Do you tithe?" he asked.

"What's that?" the lady responded.

The 86-year-old man of faith was able to explain to the financially troubled caller the principle of giving a tenth of one's income back to the Lord in obedience to the Bible (Mal. 3:10).

"I started at a young age, and God has blessed me," he told her. "You need to invest to expect."

In God's kingdom, our investments result in expectations. It's a matter of faith. We invest, and then we believe God for the return. And you can be assured that no financial statement on earth will ever reflect a greater return on investment than what we invest in His kingdom. For sure, the returns aren't always given in dollars. There are even more important returns than monetary returns. Peace. Love. Joy. Purpose. Family. Talents. The list of benefits is almost endless. But it all starts with our personal investment.

Second: *We reap in God's time.* The wisdom writer said, "There is a time for everything, and a season for every activity under heaven" (Eccles. 3:1). In the human realm, we're often on a predictable financial time clock. We live by quarterly or year-end reports. We circle April 15 on our calendars. We receive our paychecks on the 1st and the 15th or every Friday.

But God isn't necessarily on the same clock. He lives by "due time." 1 Pet. 5:6 says, "Humble yourselves, therefore, under God's mighty hand, that he may lift you up in *due time*" (emphasis added). He isn't limited by earth's time or space. He looks over the walls of calendars and planners. He sees beyond the immediate to the long range. Throughout history, His prophecies and promises have been given in "due time"—right on schedule, *His* schedule. Gal. 4:4 shows us, "When the time had fully come, God sent his Son, born of a woman, born under law." The Messiah was born right on schedule—heaven's schedule—not a moment too soon, not a moment too late.

God knows exactly what we need when we need it. We may not see an immediate return on some investment that we make in God's kingdom, but it will come right on schedule—in "due time." Our task is simply to obey His Word now and to expect the return later.

Some years ago while on a mission trip in India, we had the joy of seeing Mother Teresa in Calcutta. While there, a missionary told us the story of an assistant to Mother Teresa who was troubled because he didn't have an opportunity to speak to the saintly humanitarian. He finally arranged to talk with her during the planning of a mission trip. He told her that he would be glad to pay his own airfare for the flight if he was given an opportunity to have a few moments of her time.

Mother Teresa responded surprisingly. She advised the man that if he had enough money to purchase a ticket on the airplane, he should simply forego the trip and give the money to the poor. She told him that he would learn more from his giving than he would in spending time with her. Giving is a powerful teacher.

Jesus was the first to establish such a principle. A wealthy young man approached Him to ask the secret of a successful spiritual life. To his surprise, Jesus answered, "If you want to be perfect, go, sell your possessions and give to the poor, and you will have treasure in heaven. Then come, follow me" (Matt. 19:21). Trust doesn't carry a lot of baggage. It leans heavily on the resources of God.

Third: *We always reap more than we invest.* Jesus illustrated that principle in one of His parables, which was an example from nature that He used to teach a heavenly truth. He told of "seed [that] fell on good soil, where it produced a crop—a hundred, sixty or thirty times what was sown" (Matt. 13:8).

Another of our parishioners was a living example of the truth that Jesus taught. At the end of a sermon on giving, I promised to give people their money back in 90 days if they found that God didn't bless their tithing. Good ol' Huston stood and said, "Pastor, I discovered the joy of giving when I was 25 years old. And you can't out-give God!"

Huston then proceeded to offer a refund to any persons who tried tithing for six months. He promised to personally give their money back if God did not out-bless them. During our seven years of ministry at the church, "Huston's Guarantee" was offered during the stewardship emphasis. Each year the inquiry was made, "Huston, is your guarantee good this year?" And each year he made the same pledge without flinching. Not surprisingly, no one ever asked him for a refund!

God Pours His Love on Us

Heaven hasn't downsized. God's resources aren't subject to budget cuts. So when you're on the expecting side of an investment, you can look for a lavish return. Jesus said, "If you then, though you are evil, know how to give good gifts to your children, how much more will your Father in heaven give the Holy Spirit to those who ask him!" (Luke 11:13). In other words, if earthly parents do their very best to meet the temporal needs of their children, how much more will your heavenly Father do in meeting your spiritual needs?

But His blessings don't end with meeting spiritual needs. He is concerned with meeting temporal needs as well. In fact, God has already lent us the raw material of life: time, health, family and friends, intelligence, skills, possessions, and so forth. We're to act responsibly in managing that "loan." This is called being a steward of His resources—stewardship.

Jesus explained the concept of stewardship in the parable of the talents. He told the story of a landowner who went on a journey, entrusting his possessions to three servants who were left behind. To the first servant he gave five talents (a talent was a large sum of money, representing a day's wage many times over), to the second he gave two talents, and to the third he gave only one.

It's intriguing to see how the servants used what had been entrusted to them. They reported to him after his return. The man with five talents invested his master's resources and returned with ten talents. The second returned with four. But the last hoarded his "loan," digging a hole and burying it (see Matt. 25:14-30). All the servants shared an opportunity. But not all of them acted with responsibility.

God is a wise Heavenly Father. He doesn't give us material possessions for our detriment. He gives for our good. In return, He expects us to handle His material blessings with a sense of responsibility.

There's an interesting story about a man who was hiking a mountain range. Coming across an old-fashioned pump, he stopped for a drink. A tin cup was tied to the pump handle. The traveler noticed a note in the cup as he untied it. He quickly took the note from the cup and read, "It is safe to drink from this well. I fixed the pump and put a new sucker washer in it.

The washer dries out, and the pump needs to be primed. Under the large white rock west of the well is a bottle of water. There's enough water in it to prime the pump, but not enough if you take a drink first. Pour a little of the water into the pump to soak the leather washer. Then pour in the rest of the water and pump fast. You will soon get water."

The note continued, "Have faith. This well won't run dry. After you've pumped all the water you want, fill the bottle back up and put it where you found it. Put this note back in the cup, and tie the cup to the handle. Another thirsty traveler will soon be along."

What a beautiful portrait of God's supply: "This well won't run dry." The Old Testament prophet Jeremiah voiced it when he penned God's words, "My people will be filled with my bounty" (Jer. 31:14).

Giving to Grow Your Faith

As Huston said with his "Huston's Guarantee," you can't out-give God. What a wonderful opportunity we have to make a spiritual and financial link of faith and trust to that supply! Jesus said, "Give, and it will be given to you. A good measure, pressed down, shaken together and running over, will be poured into your lap. For with the measure you use, it will be measured to you" (Luke 6:38).

The question is—how big is your measuring cup? What size is the spiritual container you'll use to dip into God's supply? It needs to be faith-sized. If you're going to trust God for a return on your investment, you'll need to notch up your faith. (See 2 Cor. 9:7-8.) Louisa M. R. Stead expressed it so beautifully in a hymn:

> 'Tis so sweet to trust in Jesus,
> > Just to take Him at His Word,
> Just to rest upon His promise,
> > Just to know: "Thus saith the Lord."

> Jesus, Jesus, how I trust Him!
> > How I've proved Him o'er and o'er!

Jesus, Jesus, precious Jesus!
  O for grace to trust Him more!

Yes, 'tis sweet to trust in Jesus,
  Just from sin and self to cease,
Just from Jesus simply taking
  Life and rest, and joy and peace.

I'm so glad I learned to trust Thee,
  Precious Jesus, Savior, Friend;
And I know that Thou art with me,
  Wilt be with me to the end.
                                  —Louisa M. R. Stead

You'll also need to accept the "giving challenge" that the apostle Paul gave to the New Testament Church: "As you excel in everything—in faith, in speech, in knowledge, in complete earnestness and in your love for us—see that you also excel in this grace of giving" (2 Cor. 8:7). That's a step beyond gratitude for the "raw material of life" that God has given to us. It's a commitment to give something back—to give to get to give, in a glorious cycle of giving.

The Early Church not only accepted the "giving challenge"—they committed their resources in a giving routine suggested by the apostle Paul.

"On the first day of every week, each one of you should set aside a sum of money in keeping with his income, saving it up, so that when I come no collection will have to be made" (1 Cor. 16:2). Theirs wasn't a spur-of-the-moment gift. It was planned. It was systematical. It was practical.

Systematic giving is a spiritual discipline: a predetermined amount (the tithe—one-tenth) on a predetermined schedule to a predetermined place (the storehouse—church). Just as you would go through repetitive motions in strength training, you go through repetitive motions in *spiritual* strength training.

Also, you don't have to have a lot of money to link your faith to God's supply. In fact, you can be broke and still commit a portion of your resources to God. Give your time. Give your talents. Give your encouragement to another. Give a helping hand.

Trust to live. Give proportionately. Give generously. Give faithfully. And then expect a reward. It's an economic principle of God's kingdom. He instructed in Mal. 3:10, "'Bring the whole tithe into the storehouse, that there may be food in my house. Test me in this,' says the LORD Almighty, 'and see if I will not throw open the floodgates of heaven and pour out so much blessing that you will not have room enough for it.'"

Will you dare to trust Him? Will you first commit yourself to Him? Will you give Him all of your life in return for all of His? Then will you commit your finances to Him? Will you acknowledge that He's the source of your every material blessing? Will you take Him at His word, believing that He'll reward your obedience?

If so, you've begun the cycle of victorious giving. You've taken the first of many steps in a spiritually rewarding journey.

It was another missionary convention. We had moved to Tampa, Florida, to plant a church. We were distinctly impressed of God to send $50 to the Carters, missionaries to Native Americans in Arizona, even though we didn't understand why. Linda and I examined our checkbook and found just $54. We sent the $50 anyway. The next day, I went back to the post office. To our surprise, my college roommate, J. Michael Walters, who was now a seminary student, had sent us a letter and had enclosed a love gift of $50! We've often wondered how God could move financially poor church planters to send money to financially poor missionaries—and a financially poor seminary student to send money to us. But that's how God works!

Were we surprised? Of course! We're human. In the human realm, we had encountered the blessings of a divine God. It was new territory for us. But it was a lesson that we have not forgotten. We had committed our way to the Lord. We had trusted Him. And He gave us a return on our investment that still blesses our hearts after all these years.

2

COMMIT TO GROW

Giving Reflects Our Attitudes Toward Material Things

Commit your way to the LORD; trust in him.
—Ps. 37:5

Comedian Jack Benny was known for his portrayal of the world's stingiest man. In one of his comedy routines, a robber pointed a gun at Benny and demanded, "Your money or your life!" Getting no immediate response, the robber poked Benny's ribs with the gun. Benny quickly responded, 'I'm thinking! I'm thinking!"

Benny isn't the first to make a decision about life and material possessions. In fact, some have unhesitatingly traded their very lives for silver and gold, or plastic. Jesus warned, "Watch out! Be on your guard against all kinds of greed; a man's life does not consist in the abundance of his possessions . . . where your treasure is, there your heart will be also" (Luke 12:15, 34).

True commitment is all about surrendering something for a higher good—without hesitation.

Earl and Hazel Lee said, "Commitment is more than a sentimental decision that may change one's life for a few emotion-filled days. It is a valid act of the will, changing one's whole way of life."

Reflecting on his days as a missionary in India, Earl added,

The true meaning of the word "commit" came to me as I was reading Ps. 37 in Marathi, our "stepmother" language of India. In a free translation of the Marathi, it says "Turn what you are and what you have over to God—palms down!" Suppose I hold a piece of chalk in my hand and ask you to take it. You reach out and take from my upturned hand. True commitment requires me to turn my palm over and completely drop into your hand what I hold. None of it remains in my hand.[1]

I (Linda) must admit that as a teacher, I've held a few pieces of chalk in my hand. As a Christian wife and mother, I must also admit that I have struggled with turning some things over to the Lord. However, I've discovered that in those areas in which I've made a spiritual surrender, I've gained spiritual victory.

We live in a society that makes a great comparison between what we have and what we don't have. From television and radio commercials to print and billboard ads, the message is clear: *Get all you can.* If we're not careful, that kind of thinking may creep into our spiritual beliefs as well. It was the same during the time when Jesus ministered on earth. Notice John 6:1-14:

> Some time after this, Jesus crossed to the far shore of the Sea of Galilee (that is, the Sea of Tiberias), and a great crowd of people followed him because they saw the miraculous signs he had performed on the sick. Then Jesus went up on a mountainside and sat down with his disciples. The Jewish Passover Feast was near.

> When Jesus looked up and saw a great crowd coming toward him, he said to Philip, "Where shall we buy bread for these people to eat?" He asked this only to test him, for he already had in mind what he was going to do.

> Philip answered him, "Eight months' wages would not buy enough bread for each one to have a bite!"

> Another of his disciples, Andrew, Simon Peter's brother, spoke up, "Here is a boy with five small barley loaves and two small fish, but how far will they go among so many?"

Jesus said, "Have the people sit down." There was plenty of grass in that place, and the men sat down, about five thousand of them.

Jesus then took the loaves, gave thanks, and distributed to those who were seated as much as they wanted. He did the same with the fish.

When they had all had enough to eat, he said to his disciples, "Gather the pieces that are left over. Let nothing be wasted." So they gathered them and filled twelve baskets with the pieces of the five barley loaves left over by those who had eaten.

After the people saw the miraculous sign that Jesus did, they began to say, "Surely this is the Prophet who is to come into the world."

This incident in Jesus' life is a study in contrast between the givers and takers. First we see the takers: "A great crowd of people followed him because they saw the miraculous signs he had performed." They were following Jesus because of what they thought He could do for them. Whether it was putting on a good show or healing them from some sickness or disease, they were more interested in His miracles than in His majesty.

Their attitude was in contrast to that of a little boy who brought a lunch that his mother had packed for him. I've been around sack lunches my entire teaching career. I've seen how important those bundled packages of food are to children whose tummies are growling and who need a "lunch break" from the classroom routine.

The little boy in Jesus' story didn't have a big lunch—only "five small barley loaves and two small fish." But he had a big heart. He was willing to surrender his lunch so that 5,000 other people would have lunch. As you see, the giving of what he had was the start of a great miracle. Jesus blessed his gift—and multiplied it 5,000 times over.

Jesus can't bless what we hold onto selfishly. He can bless only what we give up to Him.

The Enemy of Faith

Materialism isn't just about collecting the world's stuff. It's about thinking like the world. Materialism is an attitude—the near-obsession to possess material things. John the apostle advised Christians, "Do not love the world or anything in the world. If anyone loves the world, the love of the Father is not in him. For everything in the world—the cravings of sinful man, the lust of his eyes and the boasting of what he has and does—comes not from the Father but from the world" (1 John 2:15-16).

There's nothing intrinsically wrong with having a nice car, living in a comfortable home, or dressing in the latest fashion, unless those possessions *possess* us, unless the pursuit of those things keeps us from pursuing a deeper relationship with the Lord. That's the real danger. Materialism is an enemy of faith. It replaces eternal values with earthly *valuables* in one's heart allegiance—it considers the temporal (the temporary) more important than the eternal.

Obviously that misplaced allegiance has had its effect on the Church:

> There is cause for alarm about the current giving patterns of Christians. According to the Christian Stewardship Association (CSA), giving percentages among evangelical Christians have been declining for 30 years. Church growth analyst Win Arn has said that the average senior adult contributes seven times more than the average baby boomer or buster. If that trend continues, the witness of the Church could suffer.[2]

Jesus said, "My kingdom is not of this world" (John 18:36). So if we're copying Him (living a Christian life), we'll always make our decisions—including our financial decisions—based on the eternal effect. And that won't happen naturally. It will take effort, concentrated practice, to pursue eternal things. The natural man (1 Cor. 2:14) is inclined to think more of the "here and now" than the "by and by." He or she is naturally more concerned with accumulating than with distributing.

It's a selfishness that goes all the way back to the Garden of Eden. Adam and Eve bought the suggestions of Satan and began to focus on *goods* rather than *godliness.* And it's worth noting that they lost both as a result.

Spiritual growth includes learning to commit everything to God, including material possessions. Randy Cloud wrote about the biblical traditions that illustrate such commitment:

> In the Old Testament sacrificial system, no one was to appear before God empty-handed (Exodus 34:20*b;* Deuteronomy 16:16*b*). Those who came to worship from their homes, their vineyards, their fields, and their flocks were instructed to bring their offerings generously and faithfully. Instructions were clearly given to include those who were likely to be left out. In Deuteronomy 16:11, a list is given of those who were to be included in the celebration of the Feast of Weeks. That feast celebrated the conclusion of the harvest. It was a time to honor God with a festival of gratitude for His blessings. In the instructions given for the observance, there is an oft-overlooked dimension to the feast. The feasting and worship were to include not only the immediate family of the worshiper. They were also to include the servants, both men and women, the Levites, the aliens, the orphans, and the widows living among them.[3]

The Mark of Spiritual Maturity

People in Bible times were expected to express their commitment to God by what they gave rather than what they gained. It was to be a mark of their spiritual maturity. The standard has not changed. New Testament Christians carried on the tradition by their weekly offerings. (See 1 Cor. 16:1-3.)

At the very core of our Christian faith is the acknowledgment that all material blessings are given by God—they come to us from the storehouse of His love and compassion. He is the source. Our giving is simply the supply line that channels the blessings He has already put in reserve for us. Great missionary statesman David Livingstone wrote, "I will place no value on anything I may possess except in relation to the kingdom of Christ. I will use my possessions to promote the glory of Him to whom I owe all."

The Enemy of the Kingdom of God

To the church at Laodicea Jesus made a stinging observation: "You say, 'I am rich; I have acquired wealth and do not need a thing.' But you do not realize that you are wretched, pitiful, poor, blind and naked" (Rev. 3:17). Hoarding God's blessings instead of using them for the advancement of His kingdom results in spiritual disaster. Among the effects:

- It causes a division between the haves and the have-nots.
- It promotes selfishness rather than sacrifice.
- It results in overlooking the needs of others.
- It focuses efforts on preserving the status quo rather than expansion.

Every principle of God's Word is for our benefit—for our spiritual, emotional, physical, and financial blessing. Materialism flies in the face of God's Word. And in the process, it works against His kingdom. It fails to recognize His kingdom economy.

How can the spirit of materialism be reversed in the Kingdom? It all begins with you.

First: *Refuse to be distracted.* Jesus said, "No one who puts his hand to the plow and looks back is fit for service in the kingdom of God" (Luke 9:62). The apostle Paul's life commitment was exactly the opposite. He said, "Whatever was to my profit I now consider loss for the sake of Christ. What is more, I consider everything a loss compared to the surpassing greatness of knowing Christ Jesus my Lord, for whose sake I have lost all things. I consider them rubbish, that I may gain Christ and be found in him" (Phil. 3:7-9).

Refuse to let earthly things cloud your vision of the heavenly. Embracing material things distracts us from our real goal. It divides our attention, and it divides our allegiance as well.

The personal goal of every Christian is to "seek first the kingdom of God." That cannot be done without focus, and it certainly can't be done without enthusiasm. Tithing (returning 10 percent of our income to the Lord—Mal. 3:10) is a proven and positive way to put God's kingdom first in our finances. It's an act of commitment—of turning the palms of our hands over, in the words of Earl and Hazel Lee.

Not long ago at our church, Trinity Church of the Nazarene in Oklahoma City, Bill Burch stated, "Tithing is a practical and scriptural expression of one's total consecration to God." He's right! It's a measure of our spiritual vitality.

It's written of King Hezekiah, one of the good kings in Israel's history, "In everything that he undertook in the service of God's temple and in obedience to the law and the commands, he sought his God and worked wholeheartedly. And so he prospered" (2 Chron. 31:21). Did you notice that postscript? *And so he prospered.* His wholehearted commitment resulted in his personal and material growth. When he gave, he got; and subsequently, when he got, he gave. He was practicing the "cycle of victorious giving."

Second: *Reverse the spirit of materialism by cultivating the grace of contentment.* Satan promised Eve that if she ate the forbidden fruit in the Garden of Eden, her eyes would be opened and she would be like God. Amazing! Adam and Eve had everything they could ever want; but they wanted more. "S'mores" isn't just a snack to be eaten while sitting around the campfire; it's an attitude that can cause personal and corporate havoc. A two-car garage? Why not three? A house in the suburbs? Why not add a condo in the Caribbean? Materialism breeds discontent. In their book *The Call to Contentment: Life Lessons from the Beatitudes,* authors Norman Wilson and Jerry Brecheisen wrote, "Much of modern religion is focused on external things—doing this or that, or not doing this or that. But you can do (or not do) a hundred things and still be light years away from the Kingdom. The Bible says that man looks on the outward appearance, but God looks on the heart."[4]

True happiness is not found in "doing" or "getting." It's found in committing, in making a surrender of the things we cannot keep for the things we cannot lose—eternal things.

The writer to the Hebrews gave some excellent advice: "Keep your lives free from the love of money and be content with what you have, because God has said, 'Never will I leave you; never will I forsake you'" (Heb. 13:5). Could God be saying, "If you have Me, you have all that you'll ever need"? We think so. In fact, we know so! We've found that when we put God first in our lives, everything else falls into place. And we always have enough.

Third: *To reverse the spirit of materialism, commit to an eternal plan.* Certainly we live in the now. As we said, Jesus advised us to pray, "Give us this day our daily bread." We have daily concerns—household, career, or relationship. We provide for our families. We give our employers a full day's work. We meet the needs of those we love. It's our daily duty, lovingly accepted. But there's another dimension: the eternal. We have a spiritual obligation, a divinely appointed duty, to fulfill a higher calling. It's called a Great Commission. We read in Matt. 28:18-20, "Then Jesus came to them and said, 'All authority in heaven and on earth has been given to me. Therefore go and make disciples of all nations, baptizing them in the name of the Father and of the Son and of the Holy Spirit, and teaching them to obey everything I have commanded you. And surely I am with you always, to the very end of the age.'"

A commitment to fulfill that spiritual and eternal duty affects the rest of life. Our households become mission fields, where we sow the seeds of the gospel and nurture those for whom we're responsible. Our careers provide an income that we can utilize in building God's kingdom through the local, national, or international church. Even our relationships provide nurture and support that help us fulfill the duty of reaching our world for Christ.

We receive in order to give. Paul Cunningham recently spoke at the Southwest Oklahoma District Assembly of the

Church of the Nazarene and made this statement: "Giving is but one step in the direction of total commitment, which is the essence of holy living." Generosity is consistent with the character of the Savior. Those He called were asked to make personal commitments for the benefit of others. Jesus said, "If anyone would come after me, he must deny himself and take up his cross and follow me" (Matt. 16:24).

Our lives are God's gift to us; what we do with them is our gift to Him. One of the great incidents in the New Testament is the story of the widow who gave all she had into the treasury:

Jesus sat down opposite the place where the offerings were put and watched the crowd putting their money into the temple treasury. Many rich people threw in large amounts. But a poor widow came and put in two very small copper coins, worth only a fraction of a penny.

Calling his disciples to him, Jesus said, "I tell you the truth, this poor widow has put more into the treasury than all the others. They all gave out of their wealth; but she, out of her poverty, put in everything—all she had to live on" *(Mark 12:41-44).*

Our giving and our living go hand in hand. What we are willing to share is an indicator of what is most important to us.

The Mark of Devotion

The story is told of two pastors discussing their congregations. "Every member in my church tithes," boasted one of the pastors.

His astonished colleague replied, "Every church member gives 10 percent?"

"Well, not exactly," the pastor advised. "Only 50 percent of them put their tithe into the collection plate. God collects from the rest."

The point is this: We really can't cheat God. When we withhold from Him, we hurt ourselves.

Hoarding God's resources takes its toll. But the toll is not always financial. Our selfishness results in spiritual backsliding. It robs us of the victory that results from obedience. It keeps us from enjoying the blessing of meeting the needs of others. And it hinders the very organization that was given to help us grow in faith: the Church.

When we give our tithe, it's obvious that we've been confronted with the teachings of God's Word and have accepted our responsibility to it. The result is our witness to our devotion to the Lord Jesus Christ.

There's another result: revival. Personal spiritual renewal will come to those who are committed to growing through committing their way to the Lord.

A story in the publication *Wit & Wisdom* illustrates the advantages of trusting God in the area of our giving. A stranger came to the pastor's office of a church that was suffering under financial adversity. To the pastor's amazement, the visitor said he had been made aware of the church's need, laid a blank check on his desk, and said, "Fill in the amount—whatever you need. I'll come back later to sign it."

After the stranger left, the pastor held the check in his hands. "Doesn't that man realize we have a huge debt? He couldn't possibly mean to just fill in the whole amount." Not wanting to take advantage of the kindly stranger, the pastor wrote in a figure that represented just a portion of the church's need. Soon the visitor returned. "Where's that check? I'm here to sign it." Without any hesitation, the check was signed and handed back to the pastor.

Later, the pastor learned that the office visitor was actually a wealthy philanthropist. The church's entire debt could have been erased if he would have entered the full amount.[5]

Sowing is the key to growing, as seen in the biblical account of Abraham and Isaac. Abraham's obedience to God—his willingness to fill in an amount on God's blank check—resulted in blessings that extended to his family. "Isaac planted crops in that land and the same year reaped a hundredfold, because the LORD blessed him. The man became rich, and his wealth continued to grow until he became very wealthy" (Gen. 26:12-13).

Does every act of obedience to God result in dollars in the bank? Of course not. There are many factors that influence our income, including our skills, training, perseverance, and opportunities. But obedience does add to our spiritual wealth. We become wealthier in faith—more apt to trust God for added blessing. And we become richer in our influence.

Joseph P. Blank wrote about an Indianapolis door-to-door salesman named Herbie Worth. He enjoyed only a meager income from selling household items but was well known for his acts of giving to his neighbors, helping them with fix-up projects and running errands.

Herbie died without having any living family members to come to his funeral. Blank wrote,

> As customers and acquaintances throughout Indianapolis read Herbie's obituary in their morning paper, each one reflected on this unassuming man. Neighbors swapped stories about small acts of kindness Herbie Worth had performed. Housewives recalled his dependability in making his rounds. "He has nobody," they would say to each other. "Isn't that sad? I think I'll go to his funeral."
>
> And so that is how it came to be that on a cold February morning in 1971, over one thousand people crowded into Crown Hill Cemetery in Indianapolis to attend Herbie Worth's funeral. This modest door-to-door salesman never would have imagined how many people he influenced.[6]

A. W. Tozer wrote, "One of the world's greatest tragedies is that we allow our hearts to shrink until there is room in them for little besides ourselves." When we make a commitment to grow in our giving—to commit our way to the Lord and to trust His benefits to us in return—we are not only experiencing spiritual maturity but are also lifting the burden of others and causing growth in the kingdom of God.

What are you holding that is actually holding you? Do you have possessions that are possessing you? Then this principle in the cycle of victorious Christian giving can be life-changing. You can be freed from materialism. How? By learning to commit—by trading the things you may hold dear for something even dearer.

Remember the words of the apostle: "I consider everything a loss compared to the surpassing greatness of knowing Christ Jesus my Lord, for whose sake I have lost all things. I consider them rubbish, that I may gain Christ" (Phil. 3:8).

One act of giving will result in victorious living.

3

DELIGHT TO GIVE

Giving Is an Act of
Christian Community

Delight yourself in the LORD and he will give you the desires of your heart.
—Ps. 37:4

If you hang around our friend Steve Weber very long, you'll probably hear him say, "If you want to change what you're getting, change what you're giving."

Giving is more blessing than burden. Jesus taught it: "Give, and it will be given to you" (Luke 6:38). Untold millions of people have seconded the motion in their own lives. We doubt that you'll find anyone who expresses regret for having obeyed the principles of God's Word in giving. You will, however, find those who regret that they didn't begin earlier in their lives.

Why? God openly rewards giving, and it is reflected in our daily lives. Only a cruel earthly father would discipline a child for doing exactly as he asked. Fathers delight in the obedience of their children and usually reward them for it. If that's true in family relationships, then how much more in the relationship with our Heavenly Father!

Every act of alignment with the Father's will results in ultimate blessing. It may take discipline, and in some cases sacrifice, but the end result is always worth the effort. When you think of it, it's a challenge to give God anything. For example, if you've ever had a problem shopping for a Father's Day present for your dad, think of Adam's predicament in the Garden of Eden. What do you get someone who not only *is* everything but also *owns* everything? That combination would certainly be intimidating. But as we've discussed, the widow who gave only two small coins while others gave much more delighted her Heavenly Father. He's as concerned with the attitude of our hearts as He is the amount on our checks. And besides, the principle of the tenth (giving 10 percent of what the Lord has provided back to Him in a "tithe") puts everyone in the same "giving boat."

Giving is a delight.

Earl and Hazel Lee remind us, "Delight is an attitude of the spirit." They add, "When we delight in the Lord, we lift up our eyes with deliberate intent. It is a matter of the will, not the emotions. But it often refreshingly affects the emotions. . . . The dimension of delight is actually limitless. Like circling ripples in a lake, it reaches to the very shores of heaven."[1]

Delight in giving is also an attitude of the heart—a deliberate attitude. Resentful giving is burdensome. It drags on the spirit. Its only reward is a receipt or personal recognition. Delightful giving causes the spirit to soar. It raises its eyes above the offering plate to the heavens. And there it praises the God of grace and gifts, who spared nothing to enhance the lives of His children.

Receiving God's Goodness

It's more difficult to give something to a person who is stingy than to someone who is generous. Obviously, God isn't stingy. The apostle Paul wrote, "I urge you, therefore, to reaffirm your love for him" (2 Cor. 2:8). Our giving simply underscores our gratitude for God's lavish gifts to us. Of course, His greatest gift was that of His only Son, the Lord Jesus Christ. Through that one ultimate and unselfish act, we are all recipients of God's goodness. Grace, salvation, holiness, heaven—a cycle of endless supply began at Bethlehem with the birth of the Christ Child. "From the fullness of his grace we have all received one blessing after another" (John 1:16). Paul wrote, "In Christ all the fullness of the Deity lives in bodily form, and you have been given fullness in Christ, who is the head over every power and authority" (Col. 2:9-10). Note: "We have all received" and "you have been given." No one is left out—no child is left without a heavenly inheritance.

But there's more. The giving continues. Each new day summons a flood of God's goodness. Every breath we breathe is a silent hallelujah. And the beauty of His creation is a postcard from heaven. Mountains and meadows, streams and rivers, lakes and oceans, flowers and shrubs—each earthly scene is a reminder that God spared nothing in displaying His love for us.

What can we give Him in return? We can offer Him our worship. Jesus said through John the Revelator, "Worship him who made the heavens, the earth, the sea and the springs of water" (Rev. 14:7).

The New Testament churches of Macedonia exemplify the gift of worship in a vivid way. Paul wrote in 2 Cor. 8:1-5,

> We want you to know about the grace that God has given the Macedonian churches. Out of the most severe trial, their overflowing joy and their extreme poverty welled up in rich generosity. For I testify that they gave as much as they were able, and even beyond their ability. Entirely on their own, they urgently pleaded with us for the privilege of sharing in this service to the saints. And they did not do as we expected, but they gave themselves first to the Lord and then to us in keeping with God's will.

John F. MacArthur Jr. said of Paul's account,

> The apostle was simply hoping for a monetary offering, but the Macedonia churches gave themselves—everything they had—in an act of total dedication. This demonstrated that their first priority was to make all they owned completely available and dispensable to the Lord. Such an attitude, supported by the actual exercise of giving, is really the supreme act of worship.[2]

In fact, Paul says the giving of ourselves—our bodies, souls, and minds—to God's purpose is another way we can express our gratitude for His goodness. "I urge you, brothers, in view of God's mercy, to offer your bodies as living sacrifices, holy and pleasing to God—this is your spiritual act of worship" (Rom. 12:1). Our greatest gift to God is a surrendered heart. Our personal allegiance to His will, His Word, and His way is the best way to affirm our love to Him.

> *Laid on thine altar, O my Lord, Divine,*
> *Accept my gift this day, for Jesus' sake,*
> *I have no jewels to adorn thy shrine,*
> *No world-famed sacrifice to make;*
> *And here I bring within my trembling hands*
> *This will of mine, a thing that seemeth small:*
> *Yet thou alone canst understand*
> *That when I yield thee this, I yield thee all!*[3]

Our acts of service also express our love. From helping in a homeless shelter to serving on a local church committee to singing in a praise team to teaching a Sunday School class, our service is actually a form of worship. Along with our monetary gifts, it gives us an avenue of expressing our thankfulness to God for all His benefits to us. What we *can* do we *must* do. Mother Teresa said, "I know God will not give me anything I can't handle. I just wish that He didn't trust me with so much."

Paul also reminded the church of the delight in expressing God's faithfulness. In 2 Cor. 9:7-15 we read,

> Each man should give what he has decided in his heart to give, not reluctantly or under compulsion, for God loves a cheerful giver. And God is able to make all grace abound to you, so that in all things at all times, having all that you need, you will abound in every good work. As it is written: "He has scattered abroad his gifts to the poor; his righteousness endures forever."
>
> Now he who supplies seed to the sower and bread for food will also supply and increase your store of seed and will enlarge the harvest of your righteousness. You will be

made rich in every way so that you can be generous on every occasion, and through us your generosity will result in thanksgiving to God.

This service that you perform is not only supplying the needs of God's people but is also overflowing in many expressions of thanks to God. Because of the service by which you have proved yourselves, men will praise God for the obedience that accompanies your confession of the gospel of Christ, and for your generosity in sharing with them and with everyone else. And in their prayers for you their hearts will go out to you, because of the surpassing grace God has given you. Thanks be to God for his indescribable gift!

Giving doesn't hurt—it feels good!

Blessed to Bless

God's benefits aren't given so that we may store them in a Swiss bank account, far out of sight. They're distributed to us as a part of His great cycle of giving. He gave so that we may give. It all starts with Him. He is the giver of wealth. "Every good and perfect gift is from above, coming down from the Father of the heavenly lights, who does not change like shifting shadows" (James 1:17). God is the eternal wellspring from which all our blessings flow. From His heart of love, He gives unceasingly. And those who love Him in return will reflect that same spirit.

> *I counted all my dollars while God counted crosses,*
> *I counted gains while He counted losses;*
> *I counted my worth by the things gained in store,*
> *But He sized me up by the scars that I bore.*
> *I coveted honors and sought for degrees;*
> *He wept as He counted the hours on my knees.*
> *I never knew till one day by a grave*
> *How vain are the things that we spend life to save.*
> *I did not know till a friend went above*
> *That richest is he who is rich in God's love.*[4]

It is also true that God wants the wealth that He gives kept in circulation. The wisdom writer said mournfully, "I have seen a grievous evil under the sun: wealth hoarded to the harm of its owner" (Eccles. 5:13). God is grieved when we are like selfish children who refuse to share their candy. God gives to us so that we may give to others. Our blessings shouldn't have a long shelf life. They should be distributed while they're still fresh in our hearts! A Persian proverb says, "What I kept I lost, what I spent, I had, what I gave, I have." Only in God's economy will we be guaranteed a return on our investment. What we give only comes back to us.

The Church is a great distribution center. As the wealth of God comes flowing into the lives of the believers, it is to be shared with the needy. The Early Church practiced that important principle. Acts 2:44-45 records, "All the believers were together and had everything in common. Selling their possessions and goods, they gave to anyone as he had need." This wasn't a form of socialism—it was an evidence of salvation! They were a people who once had a great need: they needed to be saved from their sin. In appreciation for God's forgiveness and restoration in their lives—their realization of God's spiritual gift of grace—they started a cycle of giving that resulted in their meeting the temporal needs of those around them.

Talmadge Johnson spoke at our church recently and said, "The greatness of a church is determined not by what it takes in but by what it sends out." Historically, a great host of churches began as missions where people were fed and clothed and given shelter. In storefront buildings across the nation, soup, songs, and sermons were interlinked. There, where temporal and spiritual needs were met, believers organized themselves into local assemblies—and later, denominations. The cycle of giving started in the New Testament Church has continued for 20 centuries.

Giving to Change the World

It was said of the New Testament believers that they would be known as Christians by their love. Their generous consideration and affection for each other would be the mark of their faith in Christ.

The world is still looking! It wants to know if this faith of ours has "legs." Is it content to be stored behind the closed doors of the church, or is it willing to walk the "road to Jericho," eager to stop to bind the broken as the Good Samaritan did? (See Luke 10:30-37.) Is it willing to leave a blank check, as he also did, to care for the man who was beaten and bloodied by the robbers? Thankfully, the Church is answering in the positive.

Christian believers are the most generous people in the world—and rightfully so. Giving protects the Church from selfishness. Jesus didn't add any strings when He said, "Give to the one who asks you, and do not turn away from the one who wants to borrow from you" (Matt. 5:42). Christian giving is proactive. It moves quickly to meet the needs of others, just like the Master.

Steve Farrar claims that we're all basically selfish—including Christians:

> Babies are not only the cutest creatures on the face of the earth; they are by far the most selfish. . . . The way God deals with my own selfishness is to give me someone to serve who has zero interest in serving me. You can't tell me God doesn't have a sense of humor. Not too many people in the world could out-selfish me one-on-one. But every time we've had a baby, I've met my match. Each of my kids resembled me. I don't mean they looked like me, I mean they were as selfish as me. This meant that somebody in the family was going to have to grow up. Guess who was nominated?[5]

Giving to get—to give again—is an ideal way to break the shackles of selfishness. This humorous "personal journal" exemplifies it:

> *Oh, God—*
> *The bumper sticker says smile if you love Jesus;*
> *So I smiled all day long*
> *And the people thought I worked for Jimmy Carter.*
> *The bumper sticker said honk if you love Jesus;*

So I honked . . . and a policeman arrested me
For disturbing the peace in a hospital zone.
The bumper stickers said wave if you love Jesus;
So I waved both hands but lost control of the car
And crashed into the back of a Baptist bus.
Oh, God—
If I cannot smile . . . or honk . . . or wave . . .
How will Jesus know I love Him?
If you love Jesus, tithe . . . honking is too easy.[6]

"Easy-believism" is a tragic malady of the modern Church —getting something for nothing, going to church for "the show" instead of genuine worship. It's possible to raise a generation of spoiled-brat Christians who think they're owed God's blessings—when in fact nobody deserves them. As Paul commented, "I am the least of the apostles and do not even deserve to be called an apostle, because I persecuted the church of God. But by the grace of God I am what I am, and his grace to me was not without effect" (1 Cor. 15:9-10).

Hymn writer John Newton was a slave trader who was gloriously forgiven. His familiar words echo the thankfulness in his heart to God:

Amazing grace! how sweet the sound
That saved a wretch like me!
I once was lost, but now am found;
Was blind but now I see.

Giving is a wonderful way to "work out," to strengthen our faith—even as we *give it away.*

Ralph Waldo Emerson wrote, "It is one of the most beautiful compensations of this life that no man can sincerely try to help another without helping himself." Our generosity not only helps to relieve the burden of another—it also lifts our own! We're lifted by our gifts of love. That's why the ideal gift is our self—what we are and what we can do for others.

And it's the most enduring gift. You've probably heard the classic story of the tight-fisted husband who kept all his money in a jar in the pantry. Nearing death, he gave his wife orders to put his money into his casket. Following his demise, the wife—who had sacrificed all of her married life because of her husband's stingy approach to money—took the money from the jar and deposited it in her checking account. Then, in an appropriate response to his request, she wrote a check for the entire amount that was in the jar and put it into the hands of her dearly departed husband.

Giving doesn't just happen at once. It has a continual effect.

Raising the Bar

You've heard the expression "raising the bar." It refers to someone's actions that have set a standard. The actions of others will be measured by that person's actions. The "cycle of victorious giving" does just that. When we apply the principle of *giving, receiving, and giving again,* it raises the standard for other believers.

The Bible gives us this reminder: "Do not forget to do good and to share with others, for with such sacrifices God is pleased" (Heb. 13:16).

Sharing, then, is the standard. God has already "set the bar." However, His people react to His standard in different ways, raising their personal standard—setting their own giving bar. Certainly, we'll never meet the standard that God set. There's no way we can give as much as He gave. But we can give in the same way:

> Sacrificially
> Purposefully
> Lovingly
> Gladly

Sadly, some give grudgingly. Charles Swindoll wrote of a little boy with a toy that had been worn by use. After he had discarded the toy, his little sister came along and wanted to play with it. The boy took it back even though he didn't really want it. The parent had to wrestle it from him to allow his sister to play with it. Swindoll says, "That's an illustration of giving 'grudgingly.' And yet the remarkable thing is that the standard approach in fund-raising is causing people to feel forced. You see, compulsion results in reluctance. When you are compelled to do something, you are all the more reluctant to give it up."[7]

Others give out of obligation: They write the checks with their hands, but their hearts aren't in it. It's just something they feel they should do instead of something they feel like doing. There's an old saying that illustrates that kind of giving: "He who gives when he is asked has waited too long."

But there's a whole other world of giving—a giving that feels good, that warms the heart as it relieves the burden of another, a giving that wells up inside like a spiritual fountain, refreshing the soul, encouraging the spirit, and strengthening the faith. It is grace giving.

At a recent crusade in Oklahoma City Billy Graham said, "God has given us two hands—one to receive with and the other to give with. We are not cisterns made for hoarding; we are channels made for sharing." Consequently we see that both "grudge giving" and "obligatory giving" are quite unnatural. They spring from the rebellious part of our nature that we inherited as the result of Adam's sin.

"Grace giving" frees us. It's a way to counteract the awful effects of Adam's rebellion against God's laws of life and living. Money is the acid test of radical obedience and discipleship.

In one sense, you can break the cycle of despair caused by humanity's first sin, with its accompanying heartache and hurt, by your cycle of giving. By your generous giving, by your delight to give, you not only express your love to God but also express your obedience to His will and His way. You reverse the effects of sin and reinforce the effects of salvation.

My (Stan's) friend Tom Phillippe is a minister of the gospel and business entrepreneur who has used his gifts not only in pastoring, once serving as an associate evangelist for Billy Graham, but also in the corporate world. He built a health care business, Nationwide Management, that employed more than 4,000 people in 30 facilities across America. Dr. Phillippe and his wife, Joan, are also known for philanthropic ventures. Hundreds of Christian organizations have been blessed by their delight in giving.

"I learned that I was not to be a reservoir or a bucket," Phillippe is quoted in a biography written for the couple's golden wedding anniversary. "I was to be a pipeline. God would pour His blessings into my life as long as I was willing to pour them out to a lost world."[8]

"Pipeline" giving is delightful giving. It's expressed in Christian community and looks up to God. It's giving out of a heart of gratitude for God's faithfulness. It loves to give because God lovingly gave.

If anyone acknowledges that Jesus is the Son of God, God lives in him and he in God. And so we know and rely on the love God has for us. God is love. Whoever lives in love lives in God, and God in him. In this way, love is made complete among us so that we will have confidence on the day of judgment, because in this world we are like him. There is no fear in love. But perfect love drives out fear, because fear has to do with punishment. The one who fears is not made perfect in love. We love because he first loved us *(1 John 4:15-19)*.

4

REST TO INHERIT

Giving Reaps Eternal Dividends

Rest in the LORD, and wait patiently for Him; Do not fret because of him who prospers in his way, Because of the man who brings wicked schemes to pass.
—Ps. 37:7, NKJV

Many years ago while we were serving on staff with John C. Maxwell in Lancaster, Ohio, we had the joy of hearing E. Stanley Jones speak. The great missionary statesman said something so prolific that I (Stan) wrote his statement in the front of my New Testament. Here's what he said:

I am inwardly fashioned for faith, not for fear. Fear is not my native land; faith is. I am so made that worry and anxiety are sand in the machinery of life; faith is the oil. I live better by faith and confidence than by fear, doubt, and anxiety. In anxiety and worry, my being is gasping for breath—these are not my native air. But in faith and confidence, I breathe freely—these are my native air.

This is a vivid portrait of a person who has learned to trust God no matter the surroundings or circumstances. It's a trust that's built on simple obedience to the Word of God. The ultimate effect of the cycle of giving is a spiritual rest in the promises of God.

In their book *The Cycle of Victorious Living,* Earl and Hazel

Lee give a wonderful perspective on the importance of spiritual rest: "The Psalm 37 rest is an active rest. God speaks; I listen and obey. And with each new situation, I find my way through the cycle to inner rest. It is a rest from friction, not a rest from action. Major Shupp of the United States Marine Corps said, 'If we can read it, we can do it.' There is a rest in doing when it is in the Lord."[1]

The psalmist said to "wait patiently." The child of God is waiting for the final curtain. This stage of life has often been filled with hectic and horrible action. But God is in control of the last act. The ropes of the final curtain are in His hands.

Yet the waiting isn't a passive waiting. It's active. We're to be actively doing the will and work of God in anticipation of the return of His Son, the Lord Jesus Christ. As the Lees said, "There is a rest in doing when it is in the Lord."

And the *doing* results in the *inheriting*.

God's Great Promise

Spiritual "getting" is a by-product of "giving." This is seen in the writings of the Old Testament: "The Lord rewards every man for his righteousness and faithfulness" (1 Sam. 26:23). And it's seen in the writings of the New Testament: "Praise be to the God and Father of our Lord Jesus Christ! In his great mercy he has given us new birth into a living hope through the resurrection of Jesus Christ from the dead, and into an inheritance that can never perish, spoil or fade—kept in heaven for you" (1 Pet. 1:3-4).

Author and radio evangelist Norman Wilson said from the Trinity Church pulpit, "Most people in the world look to the future and see a hopeless end. The believer looks to the future and sees an endless hope." God has saved the best for last. Our spiritual sacrifice and service on earth cannot possibly compare to the eternal blessings that God has reserved for us.

It truly is a win-win situation. Think of it! Live in obedience to God's Word on earth, and you receive forgiveness, peace, joy, companionship, purpose, and supply. And at the end of your life you'll get heaven!

What a hope!

From start to finish, God has covered you with His blessing. Heb. 11:6 says, "Without faith it is impossible to please God, because anyone who comes to him must believe that he exists and that he rewards those who earnestly seek him." You've driven a spiritual stake in the ground of that promise. He rewards those who earnestly seek Him.

But don't forget the benefits "along the way." As the beloved hymn of Thomas O. Chisholm says, "Morning by morning new mercies I see." Each day is a gift from heaven, hand-delivered by God himself. And your giving is an act of opening that gift.

God is a Rewarder. He rewards you in His time. (See John 11:21.) He also rewards you in ways that are not always monetary. The psalmist wrote about it: "The LORD God is a sun and shield; the LORD bestows favor and honor; no good thing does he withhold from those whose walk is blameless" (Ps. 84:11).

Think about some of the "good things." Have you left any out? Think again. Sometimes the "good things" aren't the first that come to mind.

An embrace.

A morning kiss.

Sunrise.

Sunset.

Rain.

Sometimes the least obvious blessings are the most prized.

But even without a checkbook, you can start the cycle of victorious giving. God's rewards are not for our keeping—they're for our sharing. "Therefore, as we have opportunity, let us do good to all people, especially to those who belong to the family of believers" (Gal. 6:10).

The giving cycle can begin rather insignificantly. James S. Hewett tells of the blessing of 57 pennies that were found under a little girl's pillow when she died.

The girl wanted to enter a little Sunday school in Philadelphia years ago, and was told that there was not enough room. She began saving her pennies to "help the Sunday school have more room." Two years later she became ill and died, and they found a small pocket book under her pillow with fifty-seven pennies and a piece of paper that had the following note written very neatly: "To help build the Little Temple bigger, so more children can go to Sunday school."

The pastor told the story to his congregation, and the newspaper took the story across the country. Soon the pennies grew, and the outcome can be seen in Philadelphia today. There is a church that will seat 3,300 persons, a Temple University which accommodates thousands of students, a Temple Hospital, and a large Temple Sunday school. And it all began with fifty-seven pennies.[2]

You may have more than 57 pennies—much more. But like the little girl, your sacrificial gift—offered in a spirit of love and obedience to God—can multiply many times over. God sees it. God rewards it.

Giving Is Trusting

Prov. 19:17 teaches, "He who is kind to the poor lends to the LORD, and he will reward him for what he has done." But how do you "lend" to someone who already has everything? You simply put His resources back into circulation.

As you give to Him, He gives to others—and includes you in the cycle! No matter what the amount of your gift may be, you're still getting the best end of the deal. Giving is an act of trusting God—trusting that He'll give you a return on your investment. Why does He give you the return? So that you will continue the cycle of giving—*giving, receiving, giving again.*

His supply is endless. Act on it.

- Do you need a friend? Give friendship, and He'll give you a best friend—himself. "There is a friend who sticks closer than a brother" (Prov. 18:24).

- Do you need career incentive? Give your best effort, and He'll give you wisdom to move up the ladder. "Honor the LORD with your wealth, with the firstfruits of all your crops; then your barns will be filled to overflowing, and your vats will brim over with new wine" (Prov. 3:9-10).
- Do you seek God's blessings? Invest in the lives of others, and you'll end up with His eternal approval. "God is not unjust; he will not forget your work and the love you have shown him as you have helped his people and continue to help them" (Heb. 6:10).
- Do you want to mature spiritually? Give your heart to God, and He'll reward you with His presence. "Come near to God and he will come near to you" (James 4:8).

Your actions will cause a reaction that will bless others as well. The story is told of a construction crew who was removing trees from a parcel of land. The crew's supervisor happened to notice that one tree had a bird's nest in it. Tenderheartedly, the supervisor ordered his crew to save the tree. Weeks later he returned to the lone tree remaining on the construction site. With a front-end loader, he was hoisted up to examine the bird's nest. The tiny fledglings were gone—they had learned to fly.

The supervisor then ordered the remaining tree to be cut. As it crashed to the ground, the nest scattered around. The man spotted a piece of paper among the nest's materials. He picked it up and read it. It was from a Sunday School lesson sheet that had been discarded by the janitor of a local church. The mother bird had gathered the tiny piece to help construct the nest. It contained only four remaining words from the Scripture lesson: "He careth for you" (1 Pet. 5:7, KJV).

One man's investment of time in sparing a nest, linked to a printed promise from God's Word, resulted in the welfare of tiny nestlings that lived to take flight. It was a "cycle of victorious giving."

Giving Brings Rest

In the book *The Harder I Laugh, the Deeper I Hurt*, I (Stan) tell of a crucial time in my life when I had to trust God.

I (Stan) will never forget the day my father died. My Uncle Roy picked us up in Dad's old '59 Plymouth after school and said, "We need to go to the hospital. Your dad has been hurt in an accident."

Oddly enough, two weeks earlier, I dreamed that my dad had died. Even though it had been only a dream, I awoke shaking from head to toe, sobbing and trying to grasp what life would be like without Dad. When I saw the grim look in my uncle's eyes, I instantly recalled that feeling of panic and distress. Only 11 years old, I had never felt such devastation. Looking back, I think perhaps the Lord was using the dream to prepare me for what lay ahead.

Uncle Roy drove us to Doctor's North Hospital in Columbus, Ohio. My younger brothers and I waited in the car for about five hours while Mom shuttled in and out of the hospital. Finally a policeman came out and told us that our dad had passed away. Again I recalled that horrible dream and realized I was actually living the gut-wrenching pain I had only tasted in that nightmare two weeks before. How could I ever go back home knowing Dad wouldn't be there?

When we got home, I didn't even want to get out of the car and go into the house. My heart pounded in despair as my brothers—Terry, age nine, and Mark, age three—sobbed and clung to me in the backseat of the car. Mother was so distraught that Uncle Roy had to help her into the house. I hoped he wouldn't come back; I just wanted to disappear. But in a few moments Uncle Roy returned. At that point I knew I didn't have a choice—I would have to go back into the house.

With my brothers' arms wrapped around me, I started up the steps; but I could go no farther. Gut-wrenching agony overtook me. I collapsed and wailed in pain. I felt as if

I were lost, completely lost, on a sea of suffering. Confusion hurled itself upon me. Desperation gripped me. My 11-year-old mind couldn't fathom how this could be. How could Dad—*my dad*—be dead? We had been together just the evening before. I remembered the pleasure of his warm smile. I remembered those father-and-son wrestling matches and his assurance that he loved me with all his might. How could he be dead? *How could he?*

It simply didn't make sense. We had moved to Ohio from West Virginia so Dad wouldn't have to work in the coal mines. He suffered from black lung disease and had broken his back three times before he was 30. He had moved our family to Ohio to make life better. Now he was dead! All our hopes for a better life were gone! I didn't even feel as if we were a family anymore; I wanted to run and hide. I didn't believe I could face the pain I was feeling. Hysterically I cried out, "O God—I can't go into the house again without my daddy!"

Then I heard an almost audible voice—God's voice: "Yea, though I walk through the valley of the shadow of death . . ." (Ps. 23:4, KJV). Immediately I felt the assurance that I was not alone—the Lord was with me. I stood up, wiped my eyes, and walked into the house on my own. An amazing peace swept over my soul, a peace that gave me the courage to face the difficult days to come.[3]

It was my faith in God's promise that saw me through that terrible ordeal. God had rewarded my trust with His presence. We make choices like that almost every day—choices of whether to trust in the Lord or trust in our own efforts. Bill Hybels says,

> We choose between the right thing and the convenient thing, sticking to a conviction or caving in for the sake of comfort, greed or approval. We choose either to take a carefully thought-out risk or to crawl into a shrinking shell of safety, security, and inactivity. We choose either to believe in God and trust him, even when we do not always under-

stand his ways, or to second-guess him and cower in the corners of doubt and fear.[4]

Recently we gave $1,000 to a special cause in the church. The next week we received an unexpected check for $1,410. A coincidence? Hardly. We had taken a step of faith; we had practiced the "cycle of victorious giving." God was simply giving us a return on our investment.

Our giving helped us to grow in our faith. It added to our spiritual stability. We experienced spiritual rest. Believing that God will reward our giving actually adds to our spiritual strength. John Wesley had a simple philosophy regarding his finances: *Gain all you can, save all you can, and give all you can.* How did his philosophy affect his faith? He wrote, "What way, then, can we take that our money may not sink us to the nethermost hell? There is one way, and there is no other under heaven. If those who 'gain all they can,' and 'save all they can,' will likewise 'give all they can,' then the more they gain the more they will grow in grace, and the more treasure they will lay up in heaven."

Obeying the principles of God's Word—including the principles of giving—helps us enjoy a restful life in Christ. That doesn't mean that we'll never suffer from insomnia. And it doesn't mean that we won't have stressful situations in our lives. It simply means that we've chosen to live our lives on another level, that we've chosen not to trust in our own efforts but rather to actively trust in God's supply. The result is spiritual rest.

God has promised to reward us for our faithfulness. By our giving, we've trusted Him to deliver on His promise!

Focus On Eternity

Giving is a spiritual exercise. It's far more than writing a check or putting money into the church offering plate. It is making an investment in heaven's bank. Paul said, "To those who by persistence in doing good seek glory, honor and immortality, he will give eternal life" (Rom. 2:7). The wise and spiritual use of our money here on earth will be eternally rewarded.

With over 2,000 verses in the New Testament that deal with money, God is obviously concerned with the way we handle our finances.

Our salvation is free. Jesus paid for it with His very life. But our loyalty and service to Him does not come without a personal cost. King David put it this way: "I will not sacrifice to the LORD my God burnt offerings that cost me nothing" (2 Sam. 24:24). In other words, worship without a tangible expression of gratitude is hollow and vain.

Throughout the Bible are examples of giving to the Lord—and examples of His reward for that giving. Notice the incident in the life of Simon Peter, a follower and disciple of Jesus Christ:

> One day as Jesus was standing by the Lake of Gennesaret, with the people crowding around him and listening to the word of God, he saw at the water's edge two boats, left there by the fishermen, who were washing their nets. He got into one of the boats, the one belonging to Simon, and asked him to put out a little from shore. Then he sat down and taught the people from the boat.
>
> When he had finished speaking, he said to Simon, "Put out into deep water, and let down the nets for a catch."
>
> Simon answered, "Master, we've worked hard all night and haven't caught anything. But because you say so, I will let down the nets."
>
> When they had done so, they caught such a large number of fish that their nets began to break. So they signaled their partners in the other boat to come and help them, and they came and filled both boats so full that they began to sink *(Luke 5:1-7)*.

The cycle of giving began with a simple transaction. The disciple gave Jesus one of his boats. It resulted in a bounty of fish—more fish than the disciple had caught in all of his previous attempts.

Faith enables us to see what others cannot see.

Heartfelt giving combined with believing faith will result in a miracle—a resurrection miracle. First Cor. 15:55-57 promises, "'Where, O death, is your victory? Where, O death, is your sting?' The sting of death is sin, and the power of sin is the law. But thanks be to God! He gives us the victory through our Lord Jesus Christ."

Our neighbor Mart Green recently invited us to a preview of a film documentary he produced on the life of Jim Elliot, a young missionary who paid the cost of service to the Lord with his very life. At the premier of the documentary Mart reminded the audience that Elliot once said, "He is no fool who gives what he cannot keep to gain what he cannot lose."

That is indeed the *cycle of victorious giving.*

NOTES

Chapter 1

1. Earl and Hazel Lee, *The Cycle of Victorious Living* (Kansas City: Beacon Hill Press of Kansas City, 1995), 33.

2. Thomas G. Long, "Matthew," in *Westminster Bible Companion* (Louisville, Ky.: Westminster/John Knox Press, 1974), 75.

Chapter 2

1. Earl and Hazel Lee, *The Cycle of Victorious Living*, 25.

2. Stan Toler and Elmer Towns, *Developing a Giving Church* (Kansas City: Beacon Hill Press of Kansas City, 1999), 69.

3. Randy Cloud, *Adult Leader,* March-April-May 2003, 90.

4. Norman Wilson and Jerry Brecheisen, *The Call to Contentment: Life Lessons from the Beatitudes* (Indianapolis: Wesleyan Publishing House, 2002), 18.

5. Adapted from Donald E. and Vesta W. Mansell, "Sure as the Dawn," *Wit & Wisdom,* October 15, 1993, 14.

6. Joseph P. Blank, "Who Mourns for Herbie Worth?" *Reader's Digest,* October 2001, 132A-132H.

Chapter 3

1. Earl and Hazel Lee, *The Cycle of Victorious Living,* 39.

2. John F. MacArthur Jr., *Whose Money Is It, Anyway?* (Nashville: Word Publishing, 2000), 90-91.

3. James S. Hewett, *Illustrations Unlimited* (Wheaton, Ill.: Tyndale House Publishers, 1988), 98.

4. Quoted in Ray C. Stedman, *God's Final Word: Understanding Revelation* (Grand Rapids: Discovery House Publishers, 1991), 38.

5. Steve Farrar, *Point Man: How a Man Can Lead a Family* (Nashville: Word Publishing, 1994), 44.

6. Bruce Larson and Robert Schuller, *What God Wants to Know: Finding Your Answers in God's Vital Questions* (New York: HarperCollins, 1993), 63.

7. Charles Swindoll, *The Tale of the Tardy Oxcart: And 1,501 Other Stories* [Nashville: W Publishing, 1998], 230.

8. Jerry Brecheisen, *In Pleasant Places: Celebrating the Fiftieth Wedding Anniversary of Tom & Joan Phillippe* (Copyright Thomas E. and Joan Phillippe, 2003), 26. Used by permission.

Chapter 4

1. Earl and Hazel Lee, *The Cycle of Victorious Living*, 43.

2. James S. Hewett, *Illustrations Unlimited* (Wheaton, Ill.: Tyndale House Publishers, 1988), 462.

3. Stan Toler and Debra White Smith, *The Harder I Laugh, the Deeper I Hurt* (Kansas City: Beacon Hill Press of Kansas City, 2001), 15-16.

4. Bill Hybels, *Who Are You* (When No One's Looking)? (Downers Grove, Ill.: InterVarsity Press, 1998), 82.